A CHOICE OF SONGS

A
CHOICE OF SONGS

FROM THE VERSE OF
RUDYARD KIPLING

METHUEN & CO. LTD.
36 ESSEX STREET W.C.
LONDON

First Published in 1925

PRINTED IN GREAT BRITAIN

A CHOICE OF SONGS

In Faith and Food and Books and Friends
    Give every soul her choice;
For such as follow divers ends
    In divers lights rejoice.

There is a glory of the Sun
    ('Pity it passeth soon!)
But those whose work is nearer done
    Look, rather, towards the Moon.

There is a glory of the Moon
    When the hot hours have run,
But such as have not touched their noon
    Give worship to the Sun.

There is a glory of the Stars,
    Perfect on stilly ways;
But such as follow present wars
    Pursue a noon-tide blaze.

There is one glory in all things,
    But each must find his own
Sufficient for his reckonings,
    Which is to him alone.

CONTENTS

MR. KIPLING desires to express his thanks to the Clarendon Press for permission to include "The Roman Centurion's Song," "Runnymede," and "Big Steamers," from *The History of England*, by Rudyard Kipling and C. R. L. Fletcher, and to Messrs. Macmillan & Co. Ltd. for permission to include "The Way Through the Woods," "The Wet Litany," "A Charm," "The Return of the Children," "A Carol," "A St. Helena Lullaby," "The Children's Song," "Puck's Song," "The Power of the Dog," "The Recall," "The Land," and "My New-cut Ashlar"

A CHOICE OF SONGS

SESTINA OF THE TRAMP-ROYAL

1896

SPEAKIN' in general, I 'ave tried 'em all—
The 'appy roads that take you o'er the world.
Speakin' in general, I 'ave found them good
For such as cannot use one bed too long,
But must get 'ence, the same as I 'ave done,
An' go observin' matters till they die.

What do it matter where or 'ow we die,
So long as we've our 'ealth to watch it all—
The different ways that different things are done,
An' men an' women lovin' in this world;
Takin' our chances as they come along,
An' when they ain't, pretendin' they are good?

In cash or credit—no, it aren't no good;
You 'ave to 'ave the 'abit or you'd die,
Unless you lived your life but one day long,
Nor didn't prophesy nor fret at all,
But drew your tucker some'ow from the world,
An' never bothered what you might ha' done.

But, Gawd, what things are they I 'aven't done!
I've turned my 'and to most, an' turned it good,
In various situations round the world—
For 'im that doth not work must surely die;
But that's no reason man should labour all
'Is life on one same shift—life's none so long.

Therefore, from job to job I've moved along.
Pay couldn't 'old me when my time was done,
For something in my 'ead upset it all,
Till I 'ad dropped whatever 't was for good,
An', out at sea, be'eld the dock-lights die,
An' met my mate—the wind that tramps the world!

It's like a book, I think, this bloomin' world,
Which you can read and care for just so long,
But presently you feel that you will die
Unless you get the page you're readin' done,
An' turn another—likely not so good;
But what you're after is to turn 'em all.

Gawd bless this world! Whatever she 'ath done—
Excep' when awful long—I've found it good.
So write, before I die, "'E liked it all!"

THE NATIVE-BORN

1894

WE'VE drunk to the Queen—God bless her!—
    We've drunk to our mothers' land;
We've drunk to our English brother,
    (But he does not understand);

We've drunk to the wide creation,
  And the Cross swings low for the morn,
Last toast, and of Obligation,
  A health to the Native-born!

They change their skies above them,
  But not their hearts that roam!
We learned from our wistful mothers
  To call old England " home ";
We read of the English skylark,
  Of the spring in the English lanes,
But we screamed with the painted lories
  As we rode on the dusty plains.

They passed with their old-world legends—
  Their tales of wrong and dearth—
Our fathers held by purchase,
  But we by the right of birth:
Our heart's where they rocked our cradle,
  Our love where we spent our toil,
And our faith and our hope and our honour
  We pledge to our native soil!

I charge you charge your glasses—
  I charge you drink with me
To the men of the Four New Nations,
  And the Islands of the Sea—
To the last least lump of coral,
  That none may stand outside,
And our own good pride shall teach us
  To praise our comrade's pride.

To the hush of the breathless morning
  On the thin, tin, crackling roofs,
To the haze of the burned back-ranges
  And the dust of the shoeless hoofs—

To the risk of a death by drowning,
  To the risk of a death by drouth—
To the men of a million acres,
  To the Sons of the Golden South!

To the Sons of the Golden South (Stand up !),
  And the life we live and know,
Let a fellow sing of the little things he cares about,
If a fellow fights for the little things he cares about,
  With the weight of a single blow !

To the smoke of a hundred coasters,
  To the sheep on a thousand hills,
To the sun that never blisters,
  To the rain that never chills—
To the land of the waiting springtime,
  To our five-meal, meat-fed men,
To the tall, deep-bosomed women,
  And the children nine and ten !

And the children nine and ten (Stand up !),
  And the life we live and know,
Let a fellow sing of the little things he cares about,
If a fellow fights for the little things he cares about,
  With the weight of a two-fold blow !

To the far-flung, fenceless prairie
  Where the quick cloud-shadows trail,
To our neighbour's barn in the offing
  And the line of the new-cut rail ;
To the plough in her league-long furrow
  With the grey Lake gulls behind—
To the weight of a half-year's winter
  And the warm wet western wind !

To the home of the floods and thunder,
　To her pale dry healing blue—
To the lift of the great Cape combers,
　And the smell of the baked Karroo.
To the growl of the sluicing stamp-head—
　To the reef and the water-gold,
To the last and the largest Empire,
　To the map that is half unrolled!

To our dear dark foster-mothers,
　To the heathen songs they sung—
To the heathen speech we babbled
　Ere we came to the white man's tongue.
To the cool of our deep verandas—
　To the blaze of our jewelled main,
To the night, to the palms in the moonlight,
　And the fire-fly in the cane!

To the hearth of Our People's People—
　To her well-ploughed windy sea,
To the hush of our dread high-altar
　Where The Abbey makes us We.
To the grist of the slow-ground ages,
　To the gain that is yours and mine—
To the Bank of the Open Credit,
　To the Power-house of the Line!

We've drunk to the Queen—God bless her!
　We've drunk to our mothers' land;
We've drunk to our English brother
　(And we hope he'll understand).
We've drunk as much as we're able,
　And the Cross swings low for the morn;
Last toast—and your foot on the table!—
　A health to the Native-born!

A health to the Native-born (Stand up !),
  We're six white men arow,
All bound to sing of the little things we care about,
All bound to fight for the little things we care about,
  With the weight of a six-fold blow !
By the might of our cable-tow (Take hands !),
  From the Orkneys to the Horn
All round the world (and a little loop to pull it by),
All round the world (and a little strap to buckle it).
  A health to the Native-born !

THE ROMAN CENTURION'S SONG

(ROMAN OCCUPATION OF BRITAIN, A.D. 300)

LEGATE, I had the news last night—my cohort
    ordered home
By ship to Portus Itius and thence by road to Rome.
I've marched the companies aboard, the arms are
    stowed below :
Now let another take my sword. Command me
    not to go !

I've served in Britain forty years, from Vectis to the
    Wall
I have none other home than this, nor any life at all.
Last night I did not understand, but, now the hour
    draws near
That calls me to my native land, I feel that land is
    here.

Here where men say my name was made, here
    where my work was done,
Here where my dearest dead are laid—my wife—my
    wife and son ;
Here where time, custom, grief and toil, age, mem-
    ory, service, love,
Have rooted me in British soil. Ah, how can I
    remove ?

For me this land, that sea, these airs, those folk and
    fields suffice.
What purple Southern pomp can match our change-
    ful Northern skies,
Black with December snows unshed or pearled with
    August haze—
The clanging arch of steel-grey March, or June's
    long-lighted days ?

You'll follow widening Rhodanus till vine and olive
    lean
Aslant before the sunny breeze that sweeps Nemau-
    sus clean
To Arelate's triple gate ; but let me linger on,
Here where our stiff-necked British oaks confront
    Euroclydon.

You'll take the old Aurelian Road through shore-
    descending pines
Where, blue as any peacock's neck, the Tyrrhene
    Ocean shines.
You'll go where laurel crowns are won, but—will
    you e'er forget
The scent of hawthorn in the sun, or bracken in the
    wet ?

2

Let me work here for Britain's sake—at any task
    you will—
A marsh to drain, a road to make or native troops
    to drill.
Some Western camp (I know the Pict) or granite
    Border keep,
'Mid seas of heather derelict, where our old mess-
    mates sleep.

Legate, I come to you in tears—My cohort ordered
    home !
I've served in Britain forty years.   What should I
    do in Rome ?
Here is my heart, my soul, my mind—the only life
    I know.
I cannot leave it all behind.   Command me not to
    go !

THE EXPLORER

1898

" There's no sense in going further—it's the edge of
    cultivation,"
    So they said, and I believed 'em—broke my land
    and sowed my crop—
Built my barns and strung my fences in the little
    border station
    Tucked away below the foothills where the trails
    run out and stop.

Till a voice, as bad as Conscience, rang interminable
    changes
    On one everlasting Whisper day and night
        repeated—so :
" Something hidden. Go and find it. Go and look
    behind the Ranges—
    " Something lost behind the Ranges. Lost and
        waiting for you. Go ! "

So I went, worn out of patience ; never told my
    nearest neighbours—
    Stole away with pack and ponies—left 'em drink-
        ing in the town ;
And the faith that moveth mountains didn't seem
    to help my labours
    As I faced the sheer main-ranges, whipping up
        and leading down.

March by march I puzzled through 'em, turning
    flanks and dodging shoulders,
    Hurried on in hope of water, headed back for lack
        of grass ;
Till I camped above the tree-line—drifted snow and
    naked boulders—
    Felt free air astir to windward—knew I'd stumbled
        on the Pass.

'Thought to name it for the finder : but that night
    the Norther found me—
    Froze and killed the plains-bred ponies ; so I
        called the camp Despair
(It's the Railway Gap to-day, though). Then my
    Whisper waked to hound me—
    " Something lost behind the Ranges. Over
        yonder ! Go you there ! "

Then I knew, the while I doubted—knew His Hand
    was certain o'er me.
  Still—it might be self-delusion—scores of better
    men had died—
I could reach the township living, but . . . He
    knows what terror tore me . . .
  But I didn't . . . but I didn't. I went down the
    other side,

Till the snow ran out in flowers, and the flowers
    turned to aloes,
  And the aloes sprung to thickets and a brimming
    stream ran by ;
But the thickets dwined to thorn-scrub, and the
    water drained to shallows,
  And I dropped again on desert—blasted earth,
    and blasting sky. . . .

I remember lighting fires ; I remember sitting by
    'em ;
  I remember seeing faces, hearing voices, through
    the smoke ;
I remember they were fancy—for I threw a stone
    to try 'em.
  " Something lost behind the Ranges " was the
    only word they spoke.

I remember going crazy. I remember that I knew
    it
  When I heard myself hallooing to the funny folk
    I saw.
'Very full of dreams that desert, but my two legs
    took me through it . . .
  And I used to watch 'em moving with the toes
    all black and raw.

But at last the country altered—White Man's
    country past disputing—
  Rolling grass and open timber, with a hint of hills
    behind—
There I found me food and water, and I lay a week
    recruiting.
  'Got my strength and lost my nightmares.   Then
    I entered on my find.

Thence I ran my first rough survey—chose my trees
    and blazed and ringed 'em—
  Week by week I pried and sampled—week by
    week my findings grew.
Saul he went to look for donkeys, and by God he
    found a kingdom!
  But by God, who sent His Whisper, I had struck
    the worth of two!

Up along the hostile mountains, where the hair-
    poised snow-slide shivers—
  Down and through the big fat marshes that the
    virgin ore-bed stains,
Till I heard the mile-wide mutterings of unimagined
    rivers,
  And beyond the nameless timber saw illimitable
    plains!

'Plotted sites of future cities, traced the easy grades
    between 'em ;
  Watched unharnessed rapids wasting fifty thou-
    sand head an hour ;
Counted leagues of water-frontage through the axe-
    ripe woods that screen 'em—
  Saw the plant to feed a people—up and waiting
    for the power!

Well I know who'll take the credit—all the clever
    chaps that followed—
  Came, a dozen men together—never knew my
    desert-fears ;
Tracked me by the camps I'd quitted, used the
    water-holes I'd hollowed.
  They'll go back and do the talking. *They'll* be
    called the Pioneers !

They will find my sites of townships—not the cities
    that I set there.
  They will rediscover rivers—not my rivers heard
    at night.
By my own old marks and bearings they will show
    me how to get there.
  By the lonely cairns I builded they will guide my
    feet aright.

Have I named one single river ? Have I claimed
    one single acre ?
  Have I kept one single nugget—(barring sam-
    ples) ? No, not I !
Because my price was paid me ten times over by my
    Maker.
  But you wouldn't understand it. You go up and
    occupy.

Ores you'll find there ; wood and cattle ; water-
    transit sure and steady
  (That should keep the railway rates down), coal
    and iron at your doors.
God took care to hide that country till He judged
    His people ready,
  Then He chose me for His Whisper, and I've
    found it, and it's yours !

Yes, your "Never-never country"—yes, your
"edge of cultivation"
And "no sense in going further"—till I crossed
the range to see.
God forgive me! No, *I* didn't. It's God's present
to our nation.
Anybody might have found it but—His Whisper
came to Me!

THE WAY THROUGH THE WOODS

THEY shut the road through the woods
Seventy years ago.
Weather and rain have undone it again,
And now you would never know
There was once a road through the woods
Before they planted the trees.
It is underneath the coppice and heath,
And the thin anemones.
Only the keeper sees
That, where the ring-dove broods,
And the badgers roll at ease,
There was once a road through the woods.

Yet, if you enter the woods
Of a summer evening late,
When the night-air cools on the trout-ringed pools
Where the otter whistles his mate.
(They fear not men in the woods,
Because they see so few.)
You will hear the beat of a horse's feet,
And the swish of a skirt in the dew,

Steadily cantering through
The misty solitudes,
As though they perfectly knew
The old lost road through the woods. . . .
But there is no road through the woods.

THE LAST CHANTEY

1892

" And there was no more sea."

THUS said the Lord in the Vault above the Cheru-
  bim,
  Calling to the Angels and the Souls in their
    degree :
  " Lo !   Earth has passed away
  On the smoke of Judgment Day.
  That Our word may be established shall We
    gather up the sea ? "

Loud sang the souls of the jolly, jolly mariners :
  " Plague upon the hurricane that made us furl
    and flee !
  But the war is done between us,
  In the deep the Lord hath seen us—
  Our bones we'll leave the barracout', and God
    may sink the sea ! "

Then said the soul of Judas that betrayèd Him :
  " Lord, hast Thou forgotten Thy covenant with
    me ?

How once a year I go
To cool me on the floe?
And Ye take my day of mercy if Ye take away the
sea."

Then said the soul of the Angel of the Off-shore
Wind:
(He that bits the thunder when the bull-mouthed
breakers flee):
"I have watch and ward to keep
O'er Thy wonders on the deep,
And Ye take mine honour from me if Ye take
away the sea!"

Loud sang the souls of the jolly, jolly mariners:
"Nay, but we were angry, and a hasty folk are
we.
If we worked the ship together
Till she foundered in foul weather,
Are we babes that we should clamour for a ven-
geance on the sea?"

Then said the souls of the slaves that men threw
overboard:
"Kennelled in the picaroon a weary band were
we;
But Thy arm was strong to save,
And it touched us on the wave,
And we drowsed the long tides idle till Thy
Trumpets tore the sea."

Then cried the soul of the stout Apostle Paul to
God:
"Once we frapped a ship, and she laboured
woundily.

There were fourteen score of these,
And they blessed Thee on their knees,
When they learned Thy Grace and Glory under
Malta by the sea ! "

Loud sang the souls of the jolly, jolly mariners,
Plucking at their harps, and they plucked un-
handily :
" Our thumbs are rough and tarred,
And the tune is something hard—
May we lift a Deepsea Chantey such as seamen
use at sea ? "

Then said the souls of the gentlemen-adventurers—
Fettered wrist to bar all for red iniquity :
" Ho, we revel in our chains
O'er the sorrow that was Spain's ;
Heave or sink it, leave or drink it, we were
masters of the sea ! "

Up spake the soul of a grey Gothavn 'speck-
shioner—
(He that led the flenching in the fleets of fair
Dundee) :
" Oh, the ice-blink white and near,
And the bowhead breaching clear !
Will Ye whelm them all for wantonness that
wallow in the sea ? "

Loud sang the souls of the jolly, jolly mariners,
Crying : " Under Heaven, here is neither lead
nor lee !
Must we sing for evermore
On the windless, glassy floor ?
Take back your golden fiddles and we'll beat to
open sea ! "

Then stooped the Lord, and He called the good sea
    up to Him,
  And 'stablishèd its borders unto all eternity,
    That such as have no pleasure
    For to praise the Lord by measure,
  They may enter into galleons and serve Him on
    the sea.

Sun, Wind, and Cloud shall fail not from the face of it,
  Stinging, ringing spindrift, nor the fulmar flying
    free ;
    And the ships shall go abroad
    To the Glory of the Lord
  Who heard the silly sailor-folk and gave them back
    their sea !

THE WET LITANY

WHEN the water's countenance
Blurrs 'twixt glance and second glance ;
When our tattered smokes forerun
Ashen 'neath a silvered sun ;
When the curtain of the haze
Shuts upon our helpless ways—
    Hear the Channel Fleet at sea :
    Libera nos Domine !

When the engines' bated pulse
Scarcely thrills the nosing hulls ;
When the wash along the side
Sounds, a-sudden, magnified ;
When the intolerable blast
Marks each blindfold minute passed ;

When the fog-buoy's squattering flight
Guides us through the haggard night;
When the warning bugle blows;
When the lettered doorways close;
When our brittle townships press,
Impotent, on emptiness;

When the unseen leadsmen lean
Questioning a deep unseen;
When their lessened count they tell
To a bridge invisible;
When the hid and perilous
Cliffs return our cry to us;

When the treble thickness spread
Swallows up our next-ahead;
When her siren's frightened whine
Shows her sheering out of line;
When—her passage undiscerned—
We must turn where she has turned,
    Hear the Channel Fleet at sea:
    Libera nos Domine!

THE ENGLISH FLAG

1891

*Above the portico a flag-staff bearing the Union Jack,
remained fluttering in the flames for some time, but ulti-
mately when it fell the crowds rent the air with shouts, and
seemed to see significance in the incident.*

DAILY PAPERS.

WINDS of the World, give answer! They are
    whimpering to and fro—
And what should they know of England who only
    England know?—
The poor little street-bred people that vapour and
    fume and brag,
They are lifting their heads in the stillness to yelp
    at the English Flag!

Must we borrow a clout from the Boer—to plaster
    anew with dirt?
An Irish liar's bandage, or an English coward's
    shirt?
We may not speak of England; her Flag's to sell
    or share.
What is the Flag of England? Winds of the
    World, declare!

The North Wind blew:—" From Bergen my steel-
    shod vanguards go;
" I chase your lazy whalers home from the Disko
    floe.
" By the great North Lights above me I work the
    will of God,
" And the liner splits on the ice-field or the Dogger
    fills with cod.

" I barred my gates with iron, I shuttered my doors
   with flame,
" Because to force my ramparts your nutshell navies
   came.
" I took the sun from their presence, I cut them
   down with my blast,
" And they died, but the Flag of England blew free
   ere the spirit passed.

" The lean white bear hath seen it in the long, long
   Arctic nights,
" The musk-ox knows the standard that flouts the
   Northern Lights :
" What is the Flag of England ?   Ye have but my
   bergs to dare,
" Ye have but my drifts to conquer.   Go forth, for
   it is there ! "

The South Wind sighed :—" From the Virgins my
   mid-sea course was ta'en
" Over a thousand islands lost in an idle main,
" Where the sea-egg flames on the coral and the
   long-backed breakers croon
" Their endless ocean legends to the lazy, locked
   lagoon.

" Strayed amid lonely islets, mazed amid outer
   keys,
" I waked the palms to laughter—I tossed the scud
   in the breeze.
" Never was isle so little, never was sea so lone,
" But over the scud and the palm-trees an English
   flag was flown.

" I have wrenched it free from the halliards to hang
   for a wisp on the Horn ;
" I have chased it north to the Lizard—ribboned
   and rolled and torn ;
" I have spread its fold o'er the dying, adrift in a
   hopeless sea ;
" I have hurled it swift on the slaver, and seen the
   slave set free.

" My basking sunfish know it, and wheeling alba-
   tross,
" Where the lone wave fills with fire beneath the
   Southern Cross.
" What is the Flag of England ? Ye have but
   my reefs to dare,
" Ye have but my seas to furrow. Go forth, for it
   is there ! "

The East Wind roared :—" From the Kuriles, the
   Bitter Seas, I come,
" And me men call the Home-Wind, for I bring the
   English home.
" Look—look well to your shipping !   By the breath
   of my mad typhoon
" I swept your close-packed Praya and beached
   your best at Kowloon !

" The reeling junks behind me and the racing seas
   before,
" I raped your richest roadstead—I plundered
   Singapore !
" I set my hand on the Hoogli ; as a hooded snake
   she rose ;
" And I flung your stoutest steamers to roost with
   the startled crows.

" Never the lotos closes, never the wild-fowl wake,
" But a soul goes out on the East Wind that died
      for England's sake—
" Man or woman or suckling, mother or bride or
      maid—
" Because on the bones of the English the English
      Flag is stayed.

" The desert-dust hath dimmed it, the flying wild-
      ass knows,
" The scared white leopard winds it across the
      taintless snows.
" What is the Flag of England ?   Ye have but my
      sun to dare,
" Ye have but my sands to travel.   Go forth, for it
      is there ! "

The West Wind called :—" In squadrons the
      thoughtless galleons fly
" That bear the wheat and cattle lest street-bred
      people die.
" They make my might their porter, they make my
      house their path,
" Till I loose my neck from their rudder and whelm
      them all in my wrath.

" I draw the gliding fog-bank as a snake is drawn
      from the hole,
" They bellow one to the other, the frighted ship-
      bells toll,
" For day is a drifting terror till I raise the shroud
      with my breath,
" And they see strange bows above them and the
      two go locked to death.

" But whether in calm or wrack-wreath, whether
    by dark or day,
" I heave them whole to the conger or rip their
    plates away,
" First of the scattered legions, under a shrieking sky,
" Dipping between the rollers, the English Flag
    goes by.

" The dead dumb fog hath wrapped it—the frozen
    dews have kissed—
" The naked stars have seen it, a fellow-star in the
    mist.
" What is the Flag of England ? Ye have but my
    breath to dare,
" Ye have but my waves to conquer. Go forth,
    for it is there ! "

A CHARM

TAKE of English earth as much
As either hand may rightly clutch.
In the taking of it breathe
Prayer for all who lie beneath.
Not the great nor well-bespoke,
But the mere uncounted folk,
Of whose life and death is none
Report or lamentation.
    Lay that earth upon thy heart,
    And thy sickness shall depart !

It shall sweeten and make whole
Fevered breath and festered soul.
It shall mightily restrain
Over-busied hand and brain.

It shall ease thy mortal strife
'Gainst the immortal woe of life,
Till thyself, restored, shall prove
By what grace the Heavens do move.

Take of English flowers these—
Spring's full-facèd primroses,
Summer's wild wide-hearted rose,
Autumn's wall-flower of the close,
And, thy darkness to illume,
Winter's bee-thronged ivy-bloom.
Seek and serve them where they bide
From Candlemas to Christmas-tide,
   For these simples, used aright,
   Can restore a failing sight.

These shall cleanse and purify
Webbed and inward-turning eye ;
These shall show thee treasure hid,
Thy familiar fields amid ;
And reveal (which is thy need)
Every man a King indeed !

THE SONG OF THE BANJO

1894

You couldn't pack a Broadwood half a mile—
   You mustn't leave a fiddle in the damp—
You couldn't raft an organ up the Nile,
   And play it in an Equatorial swamp.
I travel with the cooking-pots and pails—
   I'm sandwiched 'tween the coffee and the pork—
And when the dusty column checks and tails,
   You should hear me spur the rearguard to a walk !

With my " *Pilly-willy-winky-winky-popp !* "
    [Oh, it's any tune that comes into my
    head !]
So I keep 'em moving forward till they drop ;
    So I play 'em up to water and to bed.

In the silence of the camp before the fight,
    When it's good to make your will and say your
    prayer,
You can hear my *strumpty-tumpty* overnight,
    Explaining ten to one was always fair.
I'm the Prophet of the Utterly Absurd,
    Of the Patently Impossible and Vain—
And when the Thing that Couldn't has occurred,
    Give me time to change my leg and go again.

    With   my   " *Tumpa - tumpa - tumpa - tumpa-
        tump !* "
        In the desert where the dung-fed camp-
        smoke curled.
    There was never voice before us till I led our
        lonely chorus,
        I—the war-drum of the White Man round
        the world !

By the bitter road the Younger Son must tread,
    Ere he win to hearth and saddle of his own,—
'Mid the riot of the shearers at the shed,
    In the silence of the herder's hut alone—
In the twilight, on a bucket upside down,
    Hear me babble what the weakest won't confess—
I am Memory and Torment—I am Town !
    I am all that ever went with evening dress !

With my " *Tunka-tunka-tunka-tunka-tunk !* "
  [So the lights—the London Lights—grow
      near and plain !]
So I rowel 'em afresh towards the Devil and
      the Flesh,
  Till I bring my broken rankers home again.

In desire of many marvels over sea,
  Where the new-raised tropic city sweats and roars,
I have sailed with Young Ulysses from the quay
  Till the anchor rumbled down on stranger shores.
He is blooded to the open and the sky,
  He is taken in a snare that shall not fail,
He shall hear me singing strongly, till he die,
  Like the shouting of a backstay in a gale.

With my " *Hya ! Heeya ! Heeya ! Hullah !
      Haul !* "
  [Oh the green that thunders aft along the
      deck !]
Are you sick o' towns and men ?   You must
      sign and sail again,
  For it's " Johnny Bowlegs, pack your kit
      and trek ! "

Through the gorge that gives the stars at noon-day
      clear—
  Up the pass that packs the scud beneath our
      wheel—
Round the bluff that sinks her thousand fathom
      sheer—
  Down the valley with our guttering brakes
      asqueal :

Where the trestle groans and quivers in the snow,
  Where the many-shedded levels loop and twine.
Hear me lead my reckless children from below
  Till we sing the Song of Roland to the pine !

  With my " *Tinka-tinka-tinka-tinka-tink !* "
    [Oh the axe has cleared the mountain,
      croup and crest !]
  And we ride the iron stallions down to drink,
    Through the cañons to the waters of the
      West !

And the tunes that mean so much to you alone—
  Common tunes that make you choke and blow
    your nose,
Vulgar tunes that bring the laugh that brings the
    groan—
  I can rip your very heartstrings out with those ;
With the feasting, and the folly, and the fun—
  And the lying, and the lusting, and the drink,
And the merry play that drops you, when you're
    done,
  To the thoughts that burn like irons if you think.

  With my " *Plunka-lunka-lunka-lunka-lunk !* "
    Here's a trifle on account of pleasure past,
  Ere the wit that made you win gives you
      eyes to see your sin
    And—the heavier repentance at the last !

Let the organ moan her sorrow to the roof—
  I have told the naked stars the Grief of Man !
Let the trumpet snare the foeman to the proof—
  I have known Defeat, and mocked it as we ran !

My bray ye may not alter nor mistake
  When I stand to jeer the fatted Soul of Things
But the Song of Lost Endeavour that I make,
  Is it hidden in the twanging of the strings ?

          With my " *Ta-ra-rara-rara-ra-ra-rrrp !* "
            [Is it naught to you that hear and pass
              me by ?]
          But the word—the word is mine, when the
            order moves the line
              And the lean, locked ranks go roaring
                down to die !

The grandam of my grandam was the Lyre—
  [O the blue below the little fisher-huts !]
That the Stealer stooping beachward filled with fire,
  Till she bore my iron head and ringing guts !
By the wisdom of the centuries I speak—
  To the tune of yestermorn I set the truth—
I, the joy of life unquestioned—I, the Greek—
  I, the everlasting Wonder-song of Youth !

          With my " *Tinka-tinka-tinka-tinka-tink !* "
            [What d' ye lack, my noble masters ?
              What d'ye lack ?]
          So I draw the world together link by link :
            Yea, from Delos up to Limerick and
              back !

THE YOUNG QUEEN

1900

(The Commonwealth of Australia, inaugurated New Year's Day, 1901)

HER hand was still on her sword-hilt, the spur was
    still on her heel.
She had not cast her harness of grey, war-dinted
    steel ;
High on her red-splashed charger, beautiful, bold,
    and browned,
Bright-eyed out of the battle, the Young Queen
    rode to be crowned.

She came to the Old Queen's presence, in the Hall
    of Our Thousand Years—
In the Hall of the Five Free Nations that are peers
    among their peers :
Royal she gave the greeting, loyal she bowed the
    head,
Crying—" Crown me, my Mother ! "   And the Old
    Queen rose and said :—

" How can I crown thee further ?   I know whose
    standard flies
Where the clean surge takes the Leeuwin or the
    coral barriers rise.
Blood of our foes on thy bridle, and speech of our
    friends in thy mouth—
How can I crown thee further, O Queen of the
    Sovereign South ?

" Let the Five Free Nations witness ! " But the
    Young Queen answered swift :—
" It shall be crown of Our crowning to hold Our
    Crown for a gift.
In the days when Our folk were feeble thy sword
    made sure Our lands :
Wherefore We come in power to take Our Crown at
    thy hands."

And the Old Queen raised and kissed her, and the
    jealous circlet prest,
Roped with the pearls of the Northland and red
    with the gold of the West,
Lit with her land's own opals, levin-hearted, alive,
And the Five-starred Cross above them, for sign of
    the Nations Five.

So it was done in the Presence—in the Hall of Our
    Thousand Years,
In the face of the Five Free Nations that have no
    peer but their peers ;
And the Young Queen out of the Southland kneeled
    down at the Old Queen's knee,
And asked for a mother's blessing on the excellent
    years to be.

And the Old Queen stooped in the stillness where
    the jewelled head drooped low :—
" Daughter no more but Sister, and doubly
    Daughter so—
Mother of many princes—and child of the child I
    bore,
What good thing shall I wish thee that I have not
    wished before ?

" Shall I give thee delight in dominion—mere pride
    of thy setting forth ?
Nay, we be women together—we know what that
    lust is worth.
Peace in thy utmost borders, and strength on a road
    untrod ?
These are dealt or diminished at the secret will of
    God.

" I have swayed troublous councils, I am wise in
    terrible things ;
Father and son and grandson, I have known the
    hearts of the Kings.
Shall I give thee my sleepless wisdom, or the gift all
    wisdom above ?
Ay, we be women together—I give thee thy people's
    love :

" Tempered, august, abiding, reluctant of prayers
    or vows,
Eager in face of peril as thine for thy mother's
    house.
God requite thee, my Sister, through the excellent
    years to be,
And make thy people to love thee as thou hast
    lovèd me ! "

THE NEUTRAL

1916

BRETHREN, how shall it fare with me
  When the war is laid aside,
If it be proven that I am he
  For whom a world has died?

If it be proven that all my good,
  And the greater good I will make,
Were purchased me by a multitude
  Who suffered for my sake?

That I was delivered by mere mankind
  Vowed to one sacrifice,
And not, as I hold them, battle-blind,
  But dying with open eyes?

That they did not ask me to draw the sword
  When they stood to endure their lot—
That they only looked to me for a word,
  And I answered I knew them not?

If it be found, when the battle clears,
  Their death has set me free,
Then how shall I live with myself through the years
  Which they have bought for me?

Brethren, how must it fare with me,
  Or how am I justified,
If it be proven that I am he
  For whom mankind has died—
If it be proven that I am he
  Who, being questioned, denied?

RUNNYMEDE

(MAGNA CHARTA, JUNE 15, 1215)

AT Runnymede, at Runnymede,
   What say the reeds at Runnymede?
The lissom reeds that give and take,
That bend so far, but never break.
They keep the sleepy Thames awake
   With tales of John at Runnymede.

At Runnymede, at Runnymede,
   Oh hear the reeds at Runnymede :—
" You mustn't sell, delay, deny,
A freeman's right or liberty,
It wakes the stubborn Englishry,
   We saw 'em roused at Runnymede !

" When through our ranks the Barons came,
With little thought of praise or blame,
But resolute to play the game,
   They lumbered up to Runnymede ;
And there they launched in solid line,
The first attack on Right Divine—
The curt, uncompromising ' Sign ! '
   That settled John at Runnymede.

" At Runnymede, at Runnymede,
Your rights were won at Runnymede !
No freeman shall be fined or bound,
   Or dispossessed of freehold ground,
Except by lawful judgment found
And passed upon him by his peers !
Forget not, after all these years,
   The Charter signed at Runnymede."

And still when Mob or Monarch lays
Too rude a hand on English ways,
The whisper wakes, the shudder plays,
   Across the reeds at Runnymede.
And Thames, that knows the moods of kings
And crowds and priests and suchlike things,
Rolls deep and dreadful as he brings
   Their warning down from Runnymede!

SUSSEX

1902

God gave all men all earth to love,
   But since our hearts are small,
Ordained for each one spot should prove
   Belovèd over all;
That, as He watched Creation's birth,
   So we, in godlike mood,
May of our love create our earth
   And see that it is good.

So one shall Baltic pines content,
   As one some Surrey glade,
Or one the palm-grove's droned lament
   Before Levuka's Trade.
Each to his choice, and I rejoice
   The lot has fallen to me
In a fair ground—in a fair ground—
   Yea, Sussex by the sea!

No tender-hearted garden crowns,
  No bosomed woods adorn
Our blunt, bow-headed, whale-backed Downs,
  But gnarled and writhen thorn—
Bare slopes where chasing shadows skim,
  And, through the gaps revealed,
Belt upon belt, the wooded, dim,
  Blue goodness of the Weald.

Clean of officious fence or hedge,
  Half-wild and wholly tame,
The wise turf cloaks the white cliff edge
  As when the Romans came.
What sign of those that fought and died
  At shift of sword and sword?
The barrow and the camp abide,
  The sunlight and the sward.

Here leaps ashore the full Sou'west
  All heavy-winged with brine,
Here lies above the folded crest
  The Channel's leaden line;
And here the sea-fogs lap and cling,
  And here, each warning each,
The sheep-bells and the ship-bells ring
  Along the hidden beach.

We have no waters to delight
  Our broad and brookless vales—
Only the dewpond on the height
  Unfed, that never fails—
Whereby no tattered herbage tells
  Which way the season flies—
Only our close-bit thyme that smells
  Like dawn in Paradise.

Here through the strong and shadeless days
  The tinkling silence thrills ;
Or little, lost, Down churches praise
  The Lord who made the hills :
But here the Old Gods guard their round,
  And, in her secret heart,
The heathen kingdom Wilfrid found
  Dreams, as she dwells, apart.

Though all the rest were all my share,
  With equal soul I'd see
Her nine-and-thirty sisters fair,
  Yet none more fair than she.
Choose ye your need from Thames to Tweed,
  And I will choose instead
Such lands as lie 'twixt Rake and Rye,
  Black Down and Beachy Head.

I will go out against the sun
  Where the rolled scarp retires,
And the Long Man of Wilmington
  Looks naked toward the shires ;
And east till doubling Rother crawls
  To find the fickle tide,
By dry and sea-forgotten walls,
  Our ports of stranded pride.

I will go north about the shaws
  And the deep ghylls that breed
Huge oaks and old, the which we hold
  No more than Sussex weed ;
Or south where windy Piddinghoe's
  Begilded dolphin veers
And red beside wide-bankèd Ouse
  Lie down our Sussex steers.

So to the land our hearts we give
  Till the sure magic strike,
And Memory, Use, and Love make live
  Us and our fields alike—
That deeper than our speech and thought,
  Beyond our reason's sway,
Clay of the pit whence we were wrought
  Yearns to its fellow-clay.

God gives all men all earth to love,
  But since man's heart is small,
Ordains for each one spot shall prove
  Belovèd over all.
Each to his choice, and I rejoice
  The lot has fallen to me
In a fair ground—in a fair ground—
  Yea, Sussex by the sea!

THE RETURN OF THE CHILDREN

NEITHER the harps nor the crowns amused, nor the
    cherubs' dove-winged races—
Holding hands forlornly the Children wandered
    beneath the Dome,
Plucking the splendid robes of the passers by, and
    with pitiful faces
Begging what Princes and Powers refused :—" Ah,
    please will you let us go home ? "

Over the jewelled floor, nigh weeping, ran to them
    Mary the Mother,
Kneeled and caressed and made promise with
    kisses, and drew them along to the gateway—

Yea, the all-iron unbribeable Door which Peter
    must guard and none other.
Straightway She took the Keys from his keeping,
    and opened and freed them straightway.

Then, to Her Son, Who had seen and smiled, She
    said : " On the night that I bore Thee,
What didst Thou care for a love beyond mine or a
    heaven that was not my arm ?
Didst Thou push from the nipple, O Child, to hear
    the angels adore Thee ?
When we two lay in the breath of the kine ? "
    And He said :—" Thou hast done no harm."

So through the Void the Children ran homeward
    merrily hand in hand,
Looking neither to left nor right where the breath-
    less Heavens stood still.
And the Guards of the Void resheathed their swords,
    for they heard the Command :
" Shall I that have suffered the Children to come
    to Me hold them against their will ? "

A CAROL

OUR Lord Who did the Ox command
    To kneel to Judah's King,
He binds His frost upon the land
    To ripen it for Spring—
To ripen it for Spring, good sirs,
    According to His Word.
Which well must be as ye can see—
    And who shall judge the Lord ?

When we poor fenmen skate the ice
  Or shiver on the wold,
We hear the cry of a single tree
  That breaks her heart in the cold—
That breaks her heart in the cold, good sirs,
  And rendeth by the board.
Which well must be as ye can see—
  And who shall judge the Lord?

Her wood is crazed and little worth
  Excepting as to burn,
That we may warm and make our mirth
  Until the Spring return—
Until the Spring return, good sirs,
  When Christians walk abroad;
Which well must be as ye can see—
  And who shall judge the Lord?

God bless the master of this house,
  And all who sleep therein!
And guard the fens from pirate folk,
  And keep us all from sin,
To walk in honesty, good sirs,
  Of thought and deed and word!
Which shall befriend our latter end. . . .
  And who shall judge the Lord?

A ST. HELENA LULLABY

How far is St. Helena from a little child at play? "
What makes you want to wander there with all the
  world between?
Oh, Mother, call your son again or else he'll run
  away.
(*No one thinks of winter when the grass is green!*)
  4

" How far is St. Helena from a fight in Paris
    street ? "
I haven't time to answer now—the men are falling
    fast.
The guns begin to thunder, and the drums begin to
    beat.
(*If you take the first step, you will take the last!*)

" How far is St Helena from the field of Auster-
    litz ? "
You couldn't hear me if I told—so loud the cannons
    roar.
But not so far for people who are living by their
    wits.
(" *Gay go up* " means " *Gay go down* " the wide
    world o'er!)

" How far is St. Helena from an Emperor of
    France ? "
I cannot see—I cannot tell—the crowns they dazzle
    so.
The Kings sit down to dinner, and the Queens stand
    up to dance.
(*After open weather you may look for snow!*)

" How far is St. Helena from the Capes of Trafal-
    gar ? "
A longish way—a longish way—with ten year more
    to run.
It's South across the water underneath a falling
    star.
(*What you cannot finish you must leave undone!*)

" How far is St. Helena from the Beresina ice ? "
An ill way—a chill way—the ice begins to crack.

But not so far for gentlemen who never took advice.
(*When you can't go forward you must e'en come
    back !*)

" How far is St. Helena from the field of Waterloo ? "
A near way—a clear way—the ship will take you
    soon.
A pleasant place for gentlemen with little left to
    do.
(*Morning never tries you till the afternoon !*)

" How far from St. Helena to the Gate of Heaven's
    Grace ? "
That no one knows—that no one knows—and no
    one ever will,
But fold your hands across your heart and cover up
    your face,
And after all your trapesings, child, lie still !

A NATIVITY

1914–18

THE Babe was laid in the Manger
    Between the gentle kine—
All safe from cold and danger—
    " But it was not so with mine,
                    (With mine !   With mine !)
" Is it well with the child, is it well ? "
    The waiting mother prayed.
" For I know not how he fell,
    And I know not where he is laid."

A Star stood forth in Heaven ;
The Watchers ran to see
The Sign of the Promise given—
 " But there comes no sign to me.
                    (To me !   To me !)
" *My* child died in the dark.
  Is it well with the child, is it well ?
There was none to tend him or mark,
  And I know not how he fell."

The Cross was raised on high ;
 The Mother grieved beside—
" But the Mother saw Him die
  And took Him when He died.
                    (He died !   He died !)
" Seemly and undefiled
  His burial-place was made—
Is it well, is it well with the child ?
  For I know not where he is laid."

On the dawning of Easter Day
 Comes Mary Magdalene ;
But the Stone was rolled away,
 And the Body was not within—
                    "(Within !   Within !)
" Ah, who will answer my word ? "
  The broken mother prayed.
" They have taken away my Lord,
  And I know not where He is laid."

.   .   .   .   .

" *The Star stands forth in Heaven.*
 The watchers watch in vain
For Sign of the Promise given
 Of peace on Earth again—
                    "(Again !   Again !)

" But I know for Whom he fell "—
   The steadfast mother smiled,
" Is it well with the child—is it well ?
      It is well—it is well with the child ! "

THE CHILDREN'S SONG

LAND of our Birth, we pledge to thee
Our love and toil in the years to be ;
When we are grown and take our place,
As men and women with our race.

Father in Heaven who lovest all,
Oh help Thy children when they call ;
That they may build from age to age,
An undefiled heritage.

Teach us to bear the yoke in youth,
With steadfastness and careful truth ;
That, in our time, Thy Grace may give
The Truth whereby the Nations live.

Teach us to rule ourselves alway,
Controlled and cleanly night and day ;
That we may bring, if need arise,
No maimed or worthless sacrifice.

Teach us to look in all our ends,
On Thee for judge, and not our friends ;
That we, with Thee, may walk uncowed
By fear or favour of the crowd.

Teach us the Strength that cannot seek,
By deed or thought, to hurt the weak ;
That, under Thee, we may possess
Man's strength to comfort man's distress.

Teach us Delight in simple things,
And Mirth that has no bitter springs;
Forgiveness free of evil done,
And Love to all men 'neath the sun!

Land of our Birth, our faith, our pride,
For whose dear sake our fathers died;
Oh Motherland, we pledge to thee,
Head, heart, and hand through the years to be!

THE MERCHANTMEN

1893

KING SOLOMON drew merchantmen,
  Because of his desire
For peacocks, apes, and ivory,
  From Tarshish unto Tyre,
With cedars out of Lebanon
  Which Hiram rafted down,
But we be only sailormen
  That use in London town.

Coastwise—cross-seas—round the world and back
    again—
  Where the flaw shall head us or the full Trade
      suits—
Plain-sail—storm-sail—lay your board and tack
    again—
  And that's the way we'll pay Paddy Doyle for his
      boots!

We bring no store of ingots,
　　Of spice or precious stones,
But what we have we gathered
　　With sweat and aching bones :
In flame beneath the tropics,
　　In frost upon the floe,
And jeopardy of every wind
　　That does between them go.

And some we got by purchase,
　　And some we had by trade,
And some we found by courtesy
　　Of pike and carronade—
At midnight, 'mid-sea meetings,
　　For charity to keep,
And light the rolling homeward-bound
　　That rode a foot too deep !

By sport of bitter weather
　　We're walty, strained, and scarred
From the kentledge on the kelson
　　To the slings upon the yard.
Six oceans had their will of us
　　To carry all away—
Our galley's in the Baltic,
　　And our boom's in Mossel Bay !

We've floundered off the Texel,
　　Awash with sodden deals,
We've slipped from Valparaiso
　　With the Norther at our heels :
We've ratched beyond the Crossets
　　That tusk the Southern Pole,
And dipped our gunnels under
　　To the dread Agulhas roll.

Beyond all outer charting
  We sailed where none have sailed,
And saw the land-lights burning
  On islands none have hailed;
Our hair stood up for wonder,
  But, when the night was done,
There danced the deep to windward
  Blue-empty 'neath the sun!

Strange consorts rode beside us
  And brought us evil luck;
The witch-fire climbed our channels,
  And flared on vane and truck:
Till, through the red tornado,
  That lashed us nigh to blind,
We saw The Dutchman plunging,
  Full canvas, head to wind!

We've heard the Midnight Leadsman
  That calls the black deep down—
Ay, thrice we've heard The Swimmer,
  The Thing that may not drown.
On frozen bunt and gasket
  The sleet-cloud drave her hosts,
When, manned by more than signed with us,
  We passed the Isle of Ghosts!

And north, amid the hummocks,
  A biscuit-toss below,
We met the silent shallop
  That frighted whalers know;
For, down a cruel ice-lane,
  That opened as he sped,
We saw dead Hendrick Hudson
  Steer, North by West, his dead.

So dealt God's waters with us
  Beneath the roaring skies,
So walked His signs and marvels
  All naked to our eyes :
But we were heading homeward
  With trade to lose or make—
Good Lord, they slipped behind us
  In the tailing of our wake !

Let go, let go the anchors ;
  Now shamed at heart are we
To bring so poor a cargo home
  That had for gift the sea !
Let go the great bow-anchor—
  Ah, fools were we and blind—
The worst we stored with utter toil,
  The best we left behind !

*Coastwise—cross-seas—round the world and back
    again,*
  Whither flaw shall fail us or the Trades drive down :
*Plain-sail—storm-sail—lay your board and tack
    again—*
  And all to bring a cargo up to London Town !

THE SONG OF DIEGO VALDEZ

1902

THE God of Fair Beginnings
  Hath prospered here my hand—
The cargoes of my lading,
  And the keels of my command.
For out of many ventures
  That sailed with hope as high,
My own have made the better trade,
  And Admiral am I.

To me my King's much honour,
  To me my people's love—
To me the pride of Princes
  And power all pride above ;
To me the shouting cities,
  To me the mob's refrain :—
"Who knows not noble Valdez,
  "Hath never heard of Spain."

But I remember comrades—
  Old playmates on new seas—
Whenas we traded orpiment
  Among the savages—
A thousand leagues to south'ard
  And thirty years removed—
They knew not noble Valdez,
  But me they knew and loved.

Then they that found good liquor,
  They drank it not alone,
And they that found fair plunder,
  They told us every one,
About our chosen islands
  Or secret shoals between,
When, weary from far voyage,
  We gathered to careen.

There burned our breaming-fagots
  All pale along the shore :
There rose our worn pavilions—
  A sail above an oar :
As flashed each yearning anchor
  Through mellow seas afire,
So swift our careless captains
  Rowed each to his desire.

Where lay our loosened harness?
   Where turned our naked feet?
Whose tavern 'mid the palm-trees?
   What quenchings of what heat?
Oh fountain in the desert!
   Oh cistern in the waste!
Oh bread we ate in secret!
   Oh cup we spilled in haste!

The youth new-taught of longing,
   The widow curbed and wan,
The goodwife proud at season,
   And the maid aware of man—
All souls unslaked, consuming,
   Defrauded in delays,
Desire not more their quittance
   Than I those forfeit days!

I dreamed to wait my pleasure
   Unchanged my spring would bide:
Wherefore, to wait my pleasure,
   I put my spring aside
Till first in face of Fortune,
   And last in mazed disdain,
I made Diego Valdez
   High Admiral of Spain.

Then walked no wind 'neath Heaven
   Nor surge that did not aid—
I dared extreme occasion,
   Nor ever one betrayed.
They wrought a deeper treason—
   (Led seas that served my needs!)
They sold Diego Valdez
   To bondage of great deeds.

The tempest flung me seaward,
  And pinned and bade me hold
The course I might not alter—
  And men esteemed me bold!
The calms embayed my quarry,
  The fog-wreath sealed his eyes;
The dawn-wind brought my topsails—
  And men esteemed me wise!

Yet, 'spite my tyrant triumphs,
  Bewildered, dispossessed—
My dream held I before me—
  My vision of my rest;
But, crowned by Fleet and People,
  And bound by King and Pope—
Stands here Diego Valdez
  To rob me of my hope.

No prayer of mine shall move him,
  No word of his set free
The Lord of Sixty Pennants
  And the Steward of the Sea.
His will can loose ten thousand
  To seek their loves again—
But not Diego Valdez,
  High Admiral of Spain.

There walks no wind 'neath Heaven
  Nor wave that shall restore
The old careening riot
  And the clamorous, crowded shore—
The fountain in the desert,
  The cistern in the waste,
The bread we ate in secret,
  The cup we spilled in haste.

Now call I to my Captains—
  For council fly the sign,
Now leap their zealous galleys,
  Twelve-oared, across the brine.
To me the straiter prison,
  To me the heavier chain—
To me Diego Valdez,
  High Admiral of Spain!

BIG STEAMERS

1914–18

" Oh, where are you going to, all you Big Steamers,
  With England's own coal, up and down the salt
    seas ? "
" We are going to fetch you your bread and your
    butter,
  Your beef, pork, and mutton, eggs, apples, and
    cheese."

" And where will you fetch it from, all you Big
    Steamers,
  And where shall I write you when you are away ? "
" We fetch it from Melbourne, Quebec, and Van-
    couver—
  Address us at Hobart, Hong-Kong, and Bom-
    bay."

" But if anything happened to all you Big Steamers,
  And suppose you were wrecked up and down the
    salt sea ? "
" Then you'd have no coffee or bacon for breakfast,
  And you'd have no muffins or toast for your tea."

" Then I'll pray for fine weather for all you Big
      Steamers,
    For little blue billows and breezes so soft."
" Oh, billows and breezes don't bother Big Steamers,
    For we're iron below and steel-rigging aloft."

" Then I'll build a new lighthouse for all you Big
      Steamers,
    With plenty wise pilots to pilot you through."
" Oh, the Channel's as bright as a ball-room already,
    And pilots are thicker than pilchards at Looe."

" Then what can I do for you, all you Big Steamers,
    Oh, what can I do for your comfort and good ? "
" Send out your big warships to watch your big
      waters,
    That no one may stop us from bringing you
      food.

" *For the bread that you eat and the biscuits you
      nibble,*
    *The sweets that you suck and the joints that you
      carve,*
They are brought to you daily by all us Big Steamers—
    And if anyone hinders our coming you'll starve ! "

PUCK'S SONG

    SEE you the ferny ride that steals
    Into the oak-woods far ?
    O that was whence they hewed the keels
    That rolled to Trafalgar.

And mark you where the ivy clings
To Bayham's mouldering walls?
O there we cast the stout railings
That stand around St. Paul's.

See you the dimpled track that runs
All hollow through the wheat?
O that was where they hauled the guns
That smote King Philip's fleet.

(Out of the Weald, the secret Weald,
Men sent in ancient years,
The horse-shoes red at Flodden Field,
The arrows at Poitiers!)

See you our little mill that clacks,
So busy by the brook?
She has ground her corn and paid her **tax**
Ever since Domesday Book.

See you our stilly woods of oak,
And the dread ditch beside?
O that was where the Saxons broke
On the day that Harold died.

See you the windy levels spread
About the gates of Rye?
O that was where the Northmen fled,
When Alfred's ships came by.

See you our pastures wide and lone,
Where the red oxen browse?
O there was a City thronged and known,
Ere London boasted a house.

And see you, after rain, the trace
Of mound and ditch and wall?
O that was a Legion's camping-place,
When Cæsar sailed from Gaul.

And see you marks that show and fade,
Like shadows on the Downs?
O they are the lines the Flint Men made,
To guard their wondrous towns.

Trackway and Camp and City lost,
Salt Marsh where now is corn—
Old Wars, old Peace, old Arts that cease,
And so was England born!

She is not any common Earth,
Water or wood or air,
But Merlin's Isle of Gramarye,
Where you and I will fare!

" THE POWER OF THE DOG "

THERE is sorrow enough in the natural way
From men and women to fill our day;
And when we are certain of sorrow in store,
Why do we always arrange for more?
Brothers and Sisters, I bid you beware
Of giving your heart to a dog to tear.

Buy a pup and your money will buy
Love unflinching that cannot lie—
Perfect passion and worship fed
By a kick in the ribs or a pat on the head.
Nevertheless it is hardly fair
To risk your heart for a dog to tear.

When the fourteen years which Nature permits
Are closing in asthma, or tumour, or fits,
And the vet's unspoken prescription runs
To lethal chambers or loaded guns,
Then you will find—it's your own affair—
But . . . you've given your heart to a dog to tear.

When the body that lived at your single will,
With its whimper of welcome, is stilled (how still !)
When the spirit that answered your every mood
Is gone—wherever it goes—for good,
You will discover how much you care,
And will give your heart to a dog to tear.

We've sorrow enough in the natural way,
When it comes to burying Christian clay.
Our loves are not given, but only lent,
At compound interest of cent per cent.
Though it is not always the case, I believe,
That the longer we've kept 'em, the more do we
    grieve :
For, when debts are payable, right or wrong,
A short-time loan is as bad as a long—
So why in—Heaven (before we are there)
Should we give our hearts to a dog to tear ?

THE SEA AND THE HILLS

1902

Who hath desired the Sea ?—the sight of salt water
    unbounded—
The heave and the halt and the hurl and the crash
    of the comber wind-hounded ?

5

The sleek-barrelled swell before storm, grey, foam-
   less, enormous, and growing—
Stark calm on the lap of the Line or the crazy-eyed
   hurricane blowing—
His Sea in no showing the same—his Sea and the
   same 'neath each showing :
      His Sea as she slackens or thrills ?
So and no otherwise—so and no otherwise—hillmen
   desire their Hills !

Who hath desired the Sea ?—the immense and
   contemptuous surges ?
The shudder, the stumble, the swerve, as the star-
   stabbing bowsprit emerges ?
The orderly clouds of the Trades, the ridged, roaring
   sapphire thereunder—
Unheralded cliff-haunting flaws and the headsail's
   low-volleying thunder—
His Sea in no wonder the same—his Sea and the
   same through each wonder :
      His Sea as she rages or stills ?
So and no otherwise—so and no otherwise—hillmen
   desire their Hills.

Who hath desired the Sea ?   Her menaces swift as
   her mercies ?
The in-rolling walls of the fog and the silver-winged
   breeze that disperses ?
The unstable mined berg going South and the
   calvings and groans that declare it—
White water half-guessed overside and the moon
   breaking timely to bare it ;
His Sea as his fathers have dared—his Sea as his
   children shall dare it :

His Sea as she serves him or kills?
So and no otherwise—so and no otherwise—hillmen
    desire their Hills.

Who hath desired the Sea? Her excellent loneli-
    ness rather
Than forecourts of kings, and her outermost pits
    than the streets where men gather
Inland, among dust, under trees—inland where the
    slayer may slay him—
Inland, out of reach of her arms, and the bosom
    whereon he must lay him—
His Sea from the first that betrayed—at the last
    that shall never betray him:
      His Sea that his being fulfils?
So and no otherwise—so and no otherwise—hillmen
    desire their Hills.

THE RECALL

I AM the land of their fathers.
In me the virtue stays.
I will bring back my children,
After certain days.

Under their feet in the grasses
My clinging magic runs.
They shall return as strangers.
They shall remain as sons.

Over their heads in the branches
Of their new-bought, ancient trees,
I weave an incantation
And draw them to my knees.

Scent of smoke in the evening,
Smell of rain in the night—
The hours, the days and the seasons,
Order their souls aright,

Till I make plain the meaning
Of all my thousand years—
Till I fill their hearts with knowledge,
While I fill their eyes with tears.

THE LAND

When Julius Fabricius, Sub-Prefect of the Weald,
In the days of Diocletian owned our Lower River-
field,
He called to him Hobdenius—a Briton of the Clay
Saying : " What about that River-pièce for layin'
in to hay ? "

And the aged Hobden answered : " I remember as
a lad.
My father told your father that she wanted dreenin'
bad.
An' the more that you neeglect her the less you'll
get her clean.
Have it jest *as* you've a mind to, but, if I was you,
I'd dreen."

So they drained it long and crossways in the lavish
Roman style—
Still we find among the river-drift their flakes of
ancient tile,

And in drouthy middle August, when the bones of
    meadows show,
We can trace the lines they followed sixteen hundred
    years ago.

Then Julius Fabricius died as even Prefects do,
And after certain centuries, Imperial Rome died too.
Then did robbers enter Britain from across the
    Northern main
And our Lower River-field was won by Ogier the
    Dane.

Well could Ogier work his war-boat—well could
    Ogier wield his brand—
Much he knew of foaming waters—not so much of
    farming land.
So he called to him a Hobden of the old unaltered
    blood,
Saying: "What about that River-piece, she
    doesn't look no good?"

And that aged Hobden answered: "'Tain't for *me*
    to interfere,
But I've known that bit o' meadow now for five
    and fifty year.
Have it *jest* as you've a mind to, but I've proved it
    time on time,
If you want to change her nature you have *got* to
    give her lime!"

Ogier sent his wains to Lewes, twenty hours'
    solemn walk,
And drew back great abundance of the cool, grey,
    healing chalk.

And old Hobden spread it broadcast, never heeding
    what was in 't.
Which is why in cleaning ditches, now and then we
    find a flint.

Ogier died. His sons grew English—Anglo-Saxon
    was their name—
Till out of blossomed Normandy another pirate
    came ;
For Duke William conquered England and divided
    with his men,
And our Lower River-field he gave to William of
    Warenne.

But the Brook (you know her habit) rose one rainy
    autumn night
And tore down sodden flitches of the bank to left
    and right.
So, said William to his Bailiff as they rode their
    dripping rounds :
" Hob, what about that River-bit—the Brook's got
    up no bounds ? "

And that aged Hobden answered : " 'Tain't my
    business to advise,
But ye might ha' known 'twould happen from the
    way the valley lies.
Where ye can't hold back the water you must try
    and save the sile.
Hev it jest as you've a *mind* to, but, if I was you,
    I'd spile ! "

They spiled along the water-course with trunks of
    willow trees,
And planks of elms behind 'em and immortal oaken
    knees.

And when the spates of Autumn whirl the gravel-
 beds away
You can see their faithful fragments iron-hard in
 iron clay.

. . . . .

Georgii Quinti Anno Sexto, I, who own the River-
 field,
Am fortified with title-deeds, attested, signed and
 sealed,
Guaranteeing me, my assigns, my executors and heirs
All sorts of powers and profits which—are neither
 mine nor theirs.

I have rights of chase and warren, as my dignity
 requires.
I can fish—but Hobden tickles. I can shoot—but
 Hobden wires.
I repair, but he reopens, certain gaps which, men
 allege,
Have been used by every Hobden since a Hobden
 swapped a hedge.

Shall I dog his morning progress o'er the track-
 betraying dew ?
Demand his dinner-basket into which my pheasant
 flew ?
Confiscate his evening faggot under which the conies
 ran,
And summons him to judgment ? I would sooner
 summons Pan.

His dead are in the churchyard—thirty generations
 laid.
Their names were old in history when Domesday
 Book was made.

And the passion and the piety and prowess of his
    line
Have seeded, rooted, fruited in some land the Law
    calls mine.

Not for any beast that burrows, not for any bird
    that flies,
Would I lose his large sound council, miss his keen
    amending eyes.
He is bailiff, woodman, wheelwright, field-surveyor,
    engineer,
And if flagrantly a poacher—'tain't for me to
    interfere.

" Hob, what about that River-bit ? " I turn to
    him again,
With Fabricius and Ogier and William of Warenne.
" Hev it jest as you've a mind to, *but* "—and here
    he takes command.
For whoever pays the taxes old Mus' Hobden owns
    the land.

" FOR TO ADMIRE "

The Injian Ocean sets an' smiles
    So sof', so bright, so bloomin' blue ;
There aren't a wave for miles an' miles
    Excep' the jiggle from the screw.
The ship is swep', the day is done,
    The bugle's gone for smoke and play ;
An' black ag'in the settin' sun
    The Lascar sings, " *Hum deckty hai !* " [1]

[1] I'm looking out.

For to admire an' for to see,
   For to be'old this world so wide—
It never done no good to me,
   But I can't drop it if I tried !

I see the sergeants pitchin' quoits,
   I 'ear the women laugh an' talk,
I spy upon the quarter-deck
   The orficers an' lydies walk.
I thinks about the things that was,
   An' leans an' looks acrost the sea,
Till, spite of all the crowded ship,
   There's no one lef' alive but me.

The things that was which I 'ave seen,
   In barrick, camp, an' action too,
I tells them over by myself,
   An' sometimes wonders if they're true
For they was odd—most awful odd—
   But all the same now they are o'er,
There must be 'eaps o' plenty such,
   An' if I wait I'll see some more.

Oh, I 'ave come upon the books,
   An' frequent broke a barrick-rule,
An' stood beside an' watched myself
   Be'avin' like a bloomin' fool.
I paid my price for findin' out,
   Nor never grutched the price I paid,
But sat in Clink without my boots,
   Admirin' 'ow the world was made.

Be'old a cloud upon the beam,
   An' 'umped above the sea appears
Old Aden, like a barrick-stove
   That no one's lit for years an' years.

I passed by that when I began,
    An' I go 'ome the road I came,
A time-expired soldier-man
    With six years' service to 'is name.

My girl she said, " Oh, stay with me ! "
    My mother 'eld me to 'er breast.
They've never written none, an' so
    They must 'ave gone with all the rest—
With all the rest which I 'ave seen
    An' found an' known an' met along.
I cannot say the things I feel,
    And so I sing my evenin' song :

For to admire an' for to see,
    For to be'old this world so wide—
It never done no good to me,
    But I can't drop it if I tried !

" MY NEW-CUT ASHLAR "

My new-cut ashlar takes the light
Where crimson-blank the windows flare
By my own work before the night,
Great Overseer, I make my prayer.

If there be good in that I wrought
Thy Hand compelled it, Master, Thine—
Where I have failed to meet Thy thought
I know, through Thee, the blame was mine.

One instant's toil to Thee denied
Stands all Eternity's offence,
Of what I did with Thee for guide
To Thee, through Thee, be excellence.

The depth and dream of my desire,
The bitter paths wherein I stray—
Thou knowest Who hast made the Fire,
Thou knowest Who hast made the Clay.

Who, lest all thought of Eden fade,
Bring'st Eden to the craftsman's brain—
Godlike to muse o'er his own Trade
And manlike stand with God again!

One stone the more swings into place
In that dread Temple of Thy worth.
It is enough that, through Thy Grace,
I saw nought common on Thy Earth.

Take not that vision from my ken—
Oh whatsoe'er may spoil or speed.
Help me to need no aid from men
That I may help such men as need!

RECESSIONAL

1897

God of our fathers, known of old,
    Lord of our far-flung battle-line,
Beneath whose awful Hand we hold
    Dominion over palm and pine—
Lord God of Hosts, be with us yet,
Lest we forget—lest we forget!

The tumult and the shouting dies;
  The Captains and the Kings depart:
Still stands Thine ancient sacrifice,
  An humble and a contrite heart.
Lord God of Hosts, be with us yet,
Lest we forget—lest we forget!

Far-called, our navies melt away;
  On dune and headland sinks the fire:
Lo, all our pomp of yesterday
  Is one with Nineveh and Tyre!
Judge of the Nations, spare us yet,
Lest we forget—lest we forget!

If, drunk with sight of power, we loose
  Wild tongues that have not Thee in awe,
Such boastings as the Gentiles use,
  Or lesser breeds without the Law—
Lord God of Hosts, be with us yet,
Lest we forget—lest we forget!

For heathen heart that puts her trust
  In reeking tube and iron shard,
All valiant dust that builds on dust,
  And guarding, calls not Thee to guard,
For frantic boast and foolish word—
Thy mercy on Thy people, Lord!

Printed in Great Britain by
Butler & Tanner Ltd.,
Frome and London